Answering Religious Error

by

John Isaac Edwards

ISBN 10: 1-58427-289-9

ISBN 13: 978-158427-289-2

Guardian of Truth Foundation
P.O. Box 9670
Bowling Green, KY 42102
1-800-428-0121
www.truthbooks.net

Table of Contents

Foreword

I was privileged to sit in a Bible class taught by the author of this handbook, "Anwering Religious Error," at the Westside church of Christ in Salem, Indiana.

John Isaac has a love for the truth, is knowledgeable, and highly motivated in teaching the truth. In my fifty years as a member of the Lord's church, I have met only a few with his zeal. I have worked alongside him for over seven years now and look forward to many more years in service to our God.

I find this material to be a ready and concise answer to most of the major religious errors in denominationalism today. It can be used in a class situation, personal study, or as a reference when studying with someone who believes any of these errors. I am sure there are false doctrines not covered in this booklet, for it would be impossible to mention every false teaching of the past, present, or future, but the ones that are mentioned are dealt a death blow by the might of the Scriptures.

John Isaac has done an excellent job in answering these errors. 1 John 4:1 states, "Beloved, believe not every spirit, but try the spirits whether they are of God: because many false prophets are gone out into the world." "Trying the spirits" is trying the teachings of the false prophets, or false teachers, that are gone out into the world. I suppose for every doctrine taught in the Scriptures, there is a perversion of that doctrine by some religious group. The doctrine of baptism need only be mentioned as evidence of this.

Error thrives on ignorance, and, when man is ignorant of God's Word, he is vulnerable prey to Satan. There are some Scriptures hard to understand as Peter states in 2 Peter 3:16, "As also in all his epistles, speaking in them of these things; in which are some things hard to be understood, which they that are unlearned and unstable wrest, as they do also the other scriptures, unto their own destruction." We can know and understand the Scriptures (Eph. 3:4). It behooves every Christian to be prepared to do battle with error, lest our lack of preparedness allow us to be swept up in error. Every error mentioned in this handbook is a wresting of the Scriptures.

John has an excellent knowledge of the Word of God and has a unique way of confronting these perverted doctrines. I agree with his teaching, and highly recommend this handbook to those arming themselves to do battle with Satan. A soldier would never think of going to battle without his weapon. Our weapon is the Word of God. He has very neatly stacked the bullets together for us. It is left up to each of us to load our weapon and fire.

Martin F. Kennedy

May, 2002

Preface

Religious error is nothing new. Jesus told the Sadducees, "Ye do err, not knowing the scriptures, nor the power of God" (Matt. 22:29). Our best line of defense against apostasy is to arm ourselves with a good knowledge of the truth. Jesus said, "And ye shall know the truth, and the truth shall make you free" (John 8:32). Knowing the truth requires study as Paul commanded, "Study to shew thyself approved unto God, a workman that needeth not to be ashamed, rightly dividing the word of truth" (2 Tim. 2:15). The only way we will know the difference between truth and error is when we have done some daily Scripture searching (Acts 17:30). May God help each of us to become so familiar with truth that, when error rears its ugly head, we will spot it a mile away!

It is not enough to just know the difference between truth and error. We must not allow religious error to go unanswered. Paul taught the Ephesians, "And have no fellowship with the unfruitful works of darkness, but rather reprove them" (Eph. 5:11). Peter penned, "But sanctify the Lord God in your hearts: and be ready always to give an answer to every man that asketh you a reason of the hope that is in you with meekness and fear" (1 Pet. 3:15). How we answer a person is also important as Paul wrote the Colossians, "Let your speech be alway with grace, seasoned with salt, that ye may know how ye ought to answer every man" (Col. 4:6).

Whenever an individual believes something to be true, it becomes their responsibility to show where the Bible says it is true. When you encounter someone who believes something contrary to what the Bible teaches, let the burden of proof rest upon him. Ask questions like: "Where is the book, chapter, and verse that teaches that?" "Where did the Lord ever say anything about that?" "Is there an example where the apostles or early church ever practiced it?"

This material was prepared in connection with a series of classes on personal evangelism to give the students more confidence in discussing the Bible with others, and was presented in adult Bible classes before the Westside church of Christ in Salem, Indiana, where the author has labored the past seven years. The material has also been presented in the Ellettsville, Indiana Preacher Training Program in the last three years, as well as in training programs to preachers in the Philippines. This handbook is offered in the sincere hope that you will find it a useful tool in answering religious error. May God bless you in standing for truth and opposing error.

John Isaac Edwards

August, 2001

Answering Religious Error

Introduction
1. Most people have wrong impressions about what the Bible teaches on a variety of subjects.
2. Matthew 22:29 records, "Jesus answered and said unto them, Ye do err, not knowing the scriptures, nor the power of God."
   a. Religious error is nothing new.
   b. Even religious leaders can be wrong, just as the Sadducees erred.
   c. A failure to know the Scriptures is often the cause of religious error.
3. We must study and learn the truth so as to know the difference between truth and error, and be ready to give answer to religious error as we confront it.
   a. 2 Tim. 2:15
   b. John 8:32
   c. 1 Pet. 3:15
   d. Col. 4:6
4. This study seeks to answer, in a simple and scriptural manner, some religious errors of our day.

Discussion

ERROR: **Baptism Is Not Essential to Salvation**

ANSWER:
I. This makes Jesus a liar, for He said that baptism is essential to salvation. "He that believeth and is baptized shall be saved; but he that believeth not shall be damned" (Mark 16:16).
II. Peter taught that baptism is "for the remission of sins" in Acts 2:38. According to Matthew 26:28, Jesus shed His blood for the same reason. If we can be saved without baptism, can we be saved without the blood of Christ?

III. John 5:24 is parallel to Mark 16:16. If we can be saved without baptism in Mark 16:16, then can we be saved without believing in John 5:24? If not, why not?

IV. Baptism is not optional, but is essential. The Lord told Saul, "Arise, and go into the city, and it shall be told thee what thou must do" (Acts 9:6). In Damascus, Saul was told, "And now why tarriest thou? Arise, and be baptized, and wash away thy sins, calling on the name of the Lord" (Acts 22:16). If a thing is a "must," then it is essential!

V. Salvation is "in Christ Jesus" (2 Tim. 2:10). According to Galatians 3:27, we are "baptized into Christ." Thus, we must be baptized to be saved.

VI. If baptism is not essential to salvation, then why does every case of conversion in the book of Acts involve folks being baptized?

VII. If this be true, then the inspired apostle Peter was wrong when he said, "The like figure whereunto even baptism doth also now save us..." (1 Pet. 3:21).

FOR CLASS DISCUSSION:

1. How would you answer one who objected to Bible baptism on the basis that the thief on the cross, as recorded in Luke 23:39-43, was saved without being baptized?

2. What would you say to one who believed he did not need to be baptized because Mark 16:16 is not in the Revised Standard Version of the Bible?

3. Suppose one said that, if baptism was really important, the Lord would have said, "He that believeth not and is not baptized shall be damned" in Mark 16:16?

ERROR: Mechanical Instruments May Be Used in Worship

ANSWER:

I. There are two kinds of music: Vocal and mechanical. The question is, "Which kind of music has the Lord authorized?"

II. God commanded the use of mechanical instruments in Old Testament worship (2 Chron. 29:25; Ps. 81:1-4). We do not live under the Old Testament, but under the New Testament (Gal. 3:23-25; Col. 2:14; Eph. 2:14-15; Heb. 8:7-9).

III. The scope of New Testament teaching is vocal music. There are a total of ten passages in the New Testament that deal with the kind of music to be used in New Testament worship (Matt. 26:30; Mark 14:26; Acts 16:25; Rom. 15:9; 1 Cor. 14:15; Eph. 5:19; Col. 3:16; Heb. 2:12; 13:15; James 5:13). All of these passages just say to sing, without a word being said about a mechanical instrument of any kind. If the Lord wanted us to play a mechanical instrument in worship, looks like He would have said something about it.

IV. The law of exclusion states: The statement or command to do one thing only authorizes the doing of the thing specified. The doing of others is, in effect, forbidden. When God told Noah to make an ark of gopher wood in Genesis 6:14, the command to use gopher wood excluded and eliminated all other kinds of wood. When the Lord commanded singing, the command to sing only authorizes vocal music. The use of mechanical instruments is, in effect, forbidden.

V. Whatever the Lord tells me to do, He tells you to do. If He tells me to sing and play a mechanical instrument, then He tells you to sing and play a mechanical instrument. Thus, to be consistent, each one of us would have to sing and play. Do you do this?

VI. Mechanical instruments of music in New Testament worship constitute an addition to the will of God and render worship vain (2 John 9; Rev. 22:18-19; Matt. 15:9).

FOR CLASS DISCUSSION:

1. How would you respond if someone said that there will be instrumental music in heaven, and it is then acceptable in the church?

2. How would you answer one who said that the Greek term *Psallo* in Ephesians 5:19 authorizes mechanical instruments in worship unto God today?

3. What if a person said that a mechanical instrument is just an aid to the singing?

ERROR: One Church Is Just as Good as Another

ANSWER:

I. The Psalmist said, "Except the Lord build the house, they labour in vain that build it..." (Ps. 127:1). The Lord's house is the Lord's church (1 Tim. 3:15). Any church other than the Lord's has an empty existence!

11

II. The Lord only promised to build one church. "I will build my church..." (Matt. 16:18). Is a church built by man as good as the church built by Christ?

III. Paul taught only one church. "There is one body..." (Eph. 4:4). The body is identified as the church in Colossians 1:24. If there is but one body and the body is the church, then how many churches are there?

IV. We can only be reconciled in one church. Reconciliation, the making of peace with God, is only possible in the one body (Eph. 2:16), the church.

V. Jesus is the Savior of only one church. Paul penned, "and he (Christ) is the saviour of the body" (Eph. 5:23). We cannot be saved outside the Lord's church.

FOR CLASS DISCUSSION:
1. How many churches are there in the world today?
2. How would you go about helping someone in locating the Lord's church?
3. How does one become a member of the one body?

ERROR: There's Nothing in a Name

ANSWER:
I. Is a family name important to you? Would you name your daughter Jezebel or your son Ahab? The church is God's family and has been named (Eph. 3:15).

II. If one name is just as good as another, then how about telling your boss to put my name on your paycheck this week? Also, men are sent to prison for signing the wrong name to a check.

III. Proverbs 22:1 says, "A good name is rather to be chosen than great riches. . . ."

IV. The church belongs to Christ and thus wears the name of Christ. He built it (Matt. 16:18), He is its Head (Eph. 5:23), and He purchased it with His blood (Acts 20:28). This is why it is identified as the church of Christ (Rom. 16:16). Why not just call the church what it is?

V. As the bride of Christ, the church wears the name of Christ (2 Cor. 11:2; Eph. 5:24-32). How would you feel if your wife decided to start wearing the name of some other man? How do you suppose the Lord feels about those who propose to be His bride, but do not wear and honor His name?

VI. The Lord named His people as individuals. Isaiah's prophecy of the new name (Isa. 56:5; 62:2; 65:15) is fulfilled in the wearing of the name "Christian" (Acts 11:26; 26:28; 1 Pet. 4:16). The name "Christian" embraces the name of Christ.
VII. Peter taught that salvation is in a name (Acts 4:12). This makes the name we wear pretty important, doesn't it?

FOR CLASS DISCUSSION:
1. The significance of a name is seen in that God changed the names of some people. Can you think of some name changes?
2. Make a list of names used in reference to the church.
3. Can you think of terms used in reference to the Lord's people as individuals?

ERROR: Salvation Is by Faith Only

ANSWER:
I.   This contradicts plain Bible teaching. James taught, "Ye see then how that by works a man is justified, and **not by faith only**" (James 2:24).
II.   If this be true, then none will be lost (Rom. 14:11).
III. John 1:12 records, "But as many as received him, to them gave he power to become the sons of God, even to them that believe on his name." Those who believe are not the sons of God; they have the power to become the sons of God. To become a son of God, you've must be born again (John 3:1-7; 1 Pet. 1:22-23), which involves being baptized into Christ (Gal. 3:27).
IV. The Scriptures teach that nothing alone saves, but that a number of things work together to bring about our salvation. We are saved by God (1 Tim. 2:3-4), Christ (Matt. 18:11), grace (Eph. 2:8), faith (John 8:24), preaching (1 Cor. 1:21), the gospel (1 Cor. 15:1-2), baptism (1 Pet. 3:21), and the list goes on. If all these things are said to save, then you can surely see that we are not saved by faith only.

FOR CLASS DISCUSSION:
1. Be prepared to show how Acts 16:30-34 will not allow faith only salvation.
2. What kind of faith did Hebrews 11 people have?
3. Many point to passages during the life of Christ as proof texts of salvation by faith only. What bearing does Hebrews 9:15-17 have on this?

ERROR: Children Are Born Sinners

ANSWER:

I.   If sins are passed from parents to children so that children are born sinners, then God is a sinner, for Adam, who "was the son of God" (Luke 3:38), sinned.

II.   God made man upright (Eccl. 7:29; Ezek. 28:15).

III.   Children are not responsible as they have no knowledge of good and evil (Deut. 1:39; Is. 7:16).

IV.   Every man is responsible for his own conduct (Deut. 24:16; Ezek. 18:20; Col. 3:25).

V.   Children are safe in God's sight, not sinners (Matt. 18:3; Mark 10:14-15).

VI.   We are not born sinners, but become sinners by choice. Man is a free moral agent and chooses either to obey or disobey God. We become guilty of sin by either doing less than what God says (James 4:17) or going beyond what God says (2 John 9). We decide.

FOR CLASS DISCUSSION:

1.   What does eating sour grapes have to do with this (Jer. 21:29-30; Ezek. 18:1-2)?

2.   One false doctrine often breeds other false doctrines. To what false teaching has this religious error given birth?

3.   How does the death of David's child show that children are safe in God's sight (2 Sam. 12:23)?

ERROR: A Christian Cannot Sin so as to Be Eternally Lost

ANSWER:

I.   The Bible says that a Christian can sin and fall away (1 John 1:8-10; Heb. 6:4-6).

II.   The Bible reveals Christians who sinned (1 Cor. 5:1-7; Acts 8:13-21).

III.   There are warnings against sinning and falling away (1 Cor. 10:12; Heb. 4:1; 12:15; James 5:12). If it's impossible for us to be lost, why these warnings?

IV.   The Bible tells us what to do when we sin (Acts 8:22-23; James 5:16; 1 John 1:9).

V.   A Christian can be lost by the same things that save him. Faith saves (John 8:24), but it can be overthrown (2 Tim. 2:18). Grace saves (Eph.

14

2:8), but we can fall from it (Gal. 5:4). The blood of Christ saves (Eph. 1:7), but we can count it an unholy thing (Heb. 10:29). Hope saves (Rom. 8:24), but we can be moved away from it (Col. 1:23). Jesus saves (Matt. 1:21), but we can deny Him (2 Pet. 2:1). The truth saves (John 8:32), but we can err from it (James 5:19). The gospel saves (Rom. 1:16), but we can forget it (1 Cor. 15:1-2). God saves (1 Tim. 2:3-4), but we can depart from Him (Heb. 3:12).

FOR CLASS DISCUSSION:
1. What does Revelation 2:10 reveal about the crown of life?
2. Can a person quit abiding in Jesus (John 15:4-6)?
3. What are some consequences of this religious error?

ERROR: The Lord's Supper May Be Observed Weekly, Monthly, Quarterly, Semi-Annually, or Annually

ANSWER:
I. Acts 20:7 records, "And upon the first day of the week, when the disciples came together to break bread. . . ." When did the disciples break bread?
II. When God told Israel, "Remember the Sabbath day, to keep it holy" (Exod. 20:8), how often did He expect the Jews to keep the Sabbath day holy?
III. A sign says, "Rotary meets here Monday 6:15." How often does the Rotary meet? When no particular Monday is specified, every Monday is implied; and when no particular Sunday is specified, every Sunday is implied!
IV. Any event that is celebrated is celebrated as often as the day rolls around. Take your birthday for example. How often do you celebrate it? It is celebrated every year, for that is as often as the day rolls around. How often does the first day of the week roll around? Inasmuch as every week has a first day, we observe the Lord's supper every first day of the week.
V. As we observe the Lord's supper, we commune with the Lord (1 Cor. 10:16). Can you imagine the Lord's people coming together upon the first day of the week and not communing with the Lord?

15

FOR CLASS DISCUSSION:
1. How would you respond to one who used 1 Corinthians 11:26 to teach that we can observe the Lord's supper whenever we want to?
2. What elements are involved in the Lord's supper, and what is the significance of these elements (Matt. 26:26-28; 1 Cor. 11:23-25)?
3. How do you know that unleavened bread would have been used in the observance of this supper (Mark 14:12-25; Exod. 12:15-20)?

ERROR: There Is No God

ANSWER:
I. Throughout the Bible, God is assumed to exist. The fourth word of the Bible is "God" (Gen. 1:1). The Psalmist said, "The fool hath said in his heart, There is no God" (Ps. 14:1). It's in God that we "live, and move, and have our being" (Acts 17:28). The fact that we live says that God is alive! You can't believe the Bible and not believe in God.
II. The human body attests to the fact that there is a God. The Psalmist said, "I will praise thee; for I am fearfully and wonderfully made..." (Ps. 139:14). Our ears are remarkable. A piano has 88 keys, but each ear has a keyboard with 1,500 keys. We can hear the blood running through our vessels. The outside of the ears can receive up to 73,700 vibrations per second. The eye can distinguish thousands of color variations and has its own light meter, wide-angle lens, and immediate focusing and living color reproduction. The eye is both a microscope and a telescope. It can look into the heavens and see a star a million miles away or inspect the smallest of seeds. The wise man said, "The hearing ear, and the seeing eye, the Lord hath made even both of them" (Prov. 20:12). The anatomy of the human body suggests there is a God and that God made man as the Bible teaches (Gen. 1:26-27; 2:7).
III. Nature must not be overlooked. "The heavens declare the glory of God; and the firmament sheweth his handywork" (Ps. 19:1). A beautiful sunset, a rose in bloom, a moonlit sky, a colorful rainbow, the mountains, a tree, a little bird, the green grass, a lake, and a warming fire all tell us there is someone bigger than any of us!

FOR CLASS DISCUSSION:
1. How would you go about trying to prove God does not exist?
2. Take a concordance and see how many times the phrase "God is" ap-

pears in the Bible. Does this say anything to you?
3. If a person told you, "There is no God. If there was a God, my mother would not have died," what would you say?

ERROR: Christ Will Come Back to Earth, Set Up His Kingdom, and Reign 1,000 Years

ANSWER:
I.   Where is the passage that says Christ will again step foot on the earth? The Bible says that we "will meet the Lord in the air" (1 Thess. 4:17). There will be no earth for Christ to come back to as, "the earth also and the works that are therein shall be burned up" (2 Pet. 3:10). Why bring Christ back to earth anyway? His work on earth is complete (John 17:4).
II. The kingdom has already been established. The kingdom was at hand in Jesus' day (Matt. 4:17). Jesus said, "That there be some of them that stand here, which shall not taste of death, till they have seen the kingdom of God come with power" (Mark 9:1). If the kingdom has not yet been set up, then there must be some pretty old people roaming the earth today! If not, why not? Some in the first century were said to be in the kingdom (Col. 1:13; Rev. 1:9). How could they have been in the kingdom, if the kingdom hasn't been established yet? Jesus received the kingdom when He "came *to* the Ancient of days" (Dan. 7:13-14). This false teaching has Christ receiving His kingdom when He comes *from* the Ancient of Days. If you can understand the difference in *to* and *from*, you should have no difficulty answering this religious error.
III. Christ is now reigning as "King of kings, and Lord of lords" (1 Tim. 6:15). When Christ comes the second time, He will not pick up His reign but will put it down (1 Cor. 15:24-25).

FOR CLASS DISCUSSION:
1. According to John 14:1-3, what will Christ do at His coming?
2. What is the kingdom (Matt. 16:18-19; Heb. 12:23, 28)?
3. If someone used Revelation 20:4-6 to teach the 1,000 year reign of Christ on earth, how would you respond?

17

ERROR: It Makes No Difference How One Worships

ANSWER:
I.   If it makes no difference, then why was there some worship God accepted and some He did not accept? Why did God accept Abel's offering, but not Cain's in Genesis 4:1-7? Why were Nadab and Abihu struck dead by God for offering strange fire in worship unto God in Leviticus 10:1-2?
II. Our worship could not be vain, if it doesn't matter how we worship. The Lord said, "But in vain they do worship me, teaching for doctrines the commandments of men" (Matt. 15:9). The fact that worship can be vain shows it does make a difference as to how one worships!
III. Jesus taught, "God is a Spirit: and they that worship him must worship him in spirit and in truth" (John 4:24). The word "must" says some things are required in order for worship to be acceptable to God.
IV. The Scriptures instruct us as to ways men worship God acceptably: Preaching and teaching (Acts 20:7), prayer (Acts 12:5), singing (Eph. 5:19), the Lord's supper (1 Cor. 11:23-29), and giving (1 Cor. 16:1-2). Why these instructions, if it makes no difference how one worships?
V.   We must abide in the doctrine of Christ (2 John 9). Thus, we do not have the right to decide how we are going to worship the Lord. To worship as we desire, without regard for the Lord's will, is to be guilty of "will worship" (Col. 2:23).

FOR CLASS DISCUSSION:
1. God has always been very specific as to how He wanted men to worship Him. How does Deuteronomy 16 show this to be the case?
2. What does it mean to worship God in spirit?
3. What is involved in worshiping God in truth?

ERROR: If I'm Sincere And Follow My Conscience God Will Save Me

ANSWER:
I.   Conscience is the moral sense within us that determines whether we consider our own conduct right or wrong. It is the feeling of pleasure when we do what we think is right, and of pain when we do what we think is wrong.

II. Our conscience is the product of what we have been taught. If a child has been taught to steal, do you think it will bother his conscience when he takes something that is not his? If a child has been taught that it is wrong to steal, do you think it will bother his conscience when he goes to take something that belongs to another? Why the difference? The two were taught differently. The first was taught wrong, but felt he was doing right because of what he had been taught to be right. This shows that conscience is not a safe guide in religion.

III. Saul is a good example of this. He was guided by his conscience (Acts 23:1), but did "many things contrary to the name of Jesus of Nazareth" (Acts 26:9).

IV. Personal feelings can lead one astray. Solomon stated, "There is a way which seemeth right unto a man, but the end thereof are the ways of death" (Prov. 14:12).

V. Our conscience is not the standard of right and wrong, the Bible is (2 Tim. 3:16-17). If we have been taught things that are not in harmony with the Word of God and follow our conscience, our conscience will urge us to do what is wrong and will keep us from doing what is right.

FOR CLASS DISCUSSION:
1. Define the word "conscience."
2. How does Jeremiah 10:23 fit in here?
3. Show from the story of Naaman in 2 Kings 5:1-14 and the rich man of Luke 12 that it doesn't matter what we think.

ERROR: **We Are All Headed to the Same Place, Just Going Different Ways**

ANSWER:
I. If this be true, then the way to heaven would be the broad way. The Lord taught otherwise, "Because strait is the gate, and narrow is the way, which leadeth unto life, and few there be that find it" (Matt. 7:14).

II. There are not many different ways; there's just one way! Jesus told Thomas, "I am the way, the truth, and the life: no man cometh unto the Father, but by me" (John 14:6). How many ways is that?

III. Get in your car and drive around a little. You'll find that all roads do not go home!

19

IV. If we are all headed to the same place, just going different ways, then one church would be just as good as another. We know this is not so for there is one church (Eph. 4:4; Col. 1:24), and the saved are in it (Acts 2:47; Eph. 5:23).

V. Only those who do the Lord's commandments will enter heaven's pearly gates. John wrote, "Blessed are they that do his commandments, that they may have right to the tree of life, and may enter in through the gates into the city" (Rev. 22:14).

FOR CLASS DISCUSSION:
1. How do the following passages refute this false doctrine (Acts 9:2; 16:17; 18:25; 19:9)?
2. Read Matthew 7:13-14 and list the two gates, two ways, two destinies, and the two groups of people.
3. Did the rich man and Lazarus go to the same place (Luke 16:19-31)?

ERROR: God Wouldn't Punish Us, He Loves Us Too Much

ANSWER:
I. It is true that God loves us (John 3:16; Rom. 5:8; 1 John 4:8). But, He does not love us so much that He will not punish us. In fact, the wise man said, "For whom the Lord loveth he correcteth..." (Prov. 3:12).

II. The Bible reveals two sides to God: Goodness and severity (Rom. 11:22). Some examples of God's severity: The God of love drove Adam and Eve out of the Garden of Eden when they ate of the forbidden fruit (Gen. 3), sent fire out of heaven to devour Nadab and Abihu for offering strange fire (Lev. 10:1-2), and struck Ananias and Sapphira dead on the spot for lying (Acts 5:1-11).

III. The Scriptures affirm there is a hell (Matt. 5:22, 29; 10:28; 23:33). The fact that there is a hell says God is severe and will not allow sinners to go unpunished.

FOR CLASS DISCUSSION:
1. How do the angels, the flood, and the cities of Sodom and Gomorrah answer this religious error (2 Pet. 2:4-9)?
2. Pick out the expressions from Hebrews 10:26-39 that show this kind of thinking to be false.
3. What happened to some of those in the Old Testament with whom God was not pleased (1 Cor. 10:1-11)?

20

ERROR: Alexander Campbell Started the Church of Christ

ANSWER:

I.   The church of Christ was in existence long before Alexander Campbell. In a cemetery next to the old Cane Ridge meeting-house in Bourbon County, Kentucky is the headstone of William Rogers with this epitaph: "BORN IN CAMPBELL CO VA. JULY 7, 1784, REMOVED WITH HIS FATHER TO CANE RIDGE BOURBON CO APR 1798. **UNITED WITH THE CHURCH OF CHRIST AT CANE RIDGE IN 1807.** DIED FEB 15, 1862. IN THE 78 YEAR OF HIS AGE." According to *The Eternal Kingdom*, by F.W. Mattox (326), the Campbell family arrived in Washington, Pennsylvania, September 29, 1809. This shows that Alexander Campbell did not start the church of Christ, for there were churches of Christ before Campbell.

II. The church of Christ is Christ founded. Jesus stated, "I will build my church..." (Matt. 16:18). He purchased the church "with his own blood" (Acts 20:28).

III. The church of Christ had its beginning on the first Pentecost following the resurrection of Christ from the dead, as recorded in Acts 2, when the apostles preached the Word of God, folks heard it, believed it and obeyed it, and "the Lord added to the church daily such as should be saved" (Acts 2:47). It is no wonder then that nearly 1800 years before Campbell, Paul could write, "The churches of Christ salute you" (Rom. 16:16).

FOR CLASS DISCUSSION:

1.   Why should a person not belong to a church started by man (Ps. 127:1; Matt. 15:13)?

2.   Why should a person be interested in becoming a member of the church of Christ?

3.   If a member of the church of Christ is not a Campbellite, then what is he?

ERROR: The Old Testament Is Still Binding

ANSWER:

I.   God never intended for the Old Testament to be a lasting arrangement. It was only temporary — till Christ came (Gal. 3:19, 16).

II. According to Galatians 3:23-25, the law of Moses was a schoolmaster

21

and we are no longer under a schoolmaster. Therefore, we are no longer under the Old Testament.

III. The following statements concerning the Old Testament show the old law is no longer binding: "Dead to the law" (Rom. 7:4), "Delivered from the law" (Rom. 7:6), "Which is done away" (2 Cor. 3:11), "Abolished" (Eph. 2:15), "Blotting out the handwriting of ordinances" (Col. 2:14), "Took it out of the way" (Col. 2:14), "Nailing it to his cross" (Col. 2:14), and "He taketh away the first" (Heb. 10:9). These words have no meaning, if the Old Testament is still in effect.

IV. If the Old Testament is still binding, Jesus could not be priest (Heb. 8:4; 7:14). Yet, the Bible teaches Christ is not only priest, but great high priest (Heb. 4:14-15). This change in the priesthood proves there has been a law change (Heb. 7:12).

FOR CLASS DISCUSSION:
1. What are some consequences of keeping the Old Testament today?
2. Read 2 Corinthians 3 and show the Old Testament is no longer binding.
3. If we're not subject to Old Testament law, then what law are we under today (1 Cor. 9:21; Gal. 6:2)?

ERROR: **There's Only One Person in the Godhead, Jesus Only**

ANSWER:
I. The Scriptures teach there are three distinct persons in the Godhead: The Father, the Son, and the Holy Spirit (Matt. 28:19; 2 Cor. 13:14; 1 Pet. 1:1-2; 1 John 5:7).
II. Genesis 1:26 records, "And God said, Let us make man in our image, after our likeness..." The words "us" and "our" indicate a plurality of persons in the Godhead.
III. If there's only one person in the Godhead, Jesus only, please answer these questions: To whom did Jesus pray (Matt. 6:9)? Who sent Jesus (John 5:30)? By whose hand was Jesus standing (Acts 7:55)? To whom did Jesus go (John 14:28)? To whom will Jesus present the kingdom (1 Cor. 15:24)? How do you explain the baptism of Jesus (Matt. 3:16-17)? Has any man ever seen Christ (John 1:18)? Is Jesus alone in the Godhead (John 8:16-17)?
IV. The number of persons in the Godhead is a simple matter of arithmetic (Eph. 4:4-6).

```
1 Body
1 Spirit ........................ 1 Spirit
1 Hope
1 Lord ......................... 1 Lord
1 Faith
1 Baptism
1 Father ....................... 1 Father
5 or 7 (circle one of these)    1 or 3 (circle one)
```

Note: If you circled 7 in column one, then you must also circle 3 in column two. If you circled 1 in column two, then you must also circle 5 in column one. The "oneness" people are in trouble either way with this passage.

FOR CLASS DISCUSSION:
1. Show that there were three persons present at the creation (Gen. 1:1-4; Col. 1:16).
2. How may the baptism of Jesus be used to answer this religious error (Matt. 3:16-17)?
3. From Philippians 2:5-11, show there is more than one person in the Godhead.

ERROR: Sprinkling or Pouring Is Sufficient for Baptism

ANSWER:
I. In order for sprinkling or pouring to be sufficient for Bible baptism, you would have to redefine the word "baptism." The English word "baptism" is a transliteration of the Greek word *baptisma*, meaning immersion, submersion, a burial, an overwhelming.
II. The Bible teaches the action of baptism is burial; not sprinkling or pouring. Observe the word "buried" in Romans 6:4 and Colossians 2:12.
III. Baptism demonstrated in the New Testament proves, beyond a shadow of a doubt, the action of Bible baptism is immersion; not sprinkling or pouring. Acts 8:36-39 reveals, "And he commanded the chariot to stand still: and they went down both into the water, both Philip and the eunuch, and he baptized him. And when they were come up out of the water. . . ." Bible baptism requires a going down into the water and a coming up out of the water. Sprinkling and pouring do not fit!

23

IV. According to Romans 6:5, baptism is a planting. When you plant a seed in the ground, do you just sprinkle or pour a little dirt over it, or do you bury it?

V. There is not an example in the New Testament of anyone ever having water sprinkled or poured on them for any purpose.

FOR CLASS DISCUSSION:

1. Why was John baptizing in Aenon near Salem (John 3:23)? Do you see any significance in that?
2. What about a man on a death bed — would it be okay to just sprinkle or pour a little water over him in place of immersing him? Why or why not?
3. Explain how baptism is a form of the death, burial, and resurrection of Christ (Rom. 6:1-7, 17-18).

ERROR: **The Lord's Supper May Be Observed Any Day of the Week**

ANSWER:

I. God has always been specific as to days. The fourth command was, "Remember the sabbath day, to keep it holy" (Exod. 20:8). The Bible mentions, "the day of Pentecost" (Acts 2:1), which came fifty days after the Passover (Lev. 23:15-16). The Israelites were not at liberty to keep these days just any day they got ready; there was a specific day set aside.

II. By apostolic example, we learn that the Lord's supper is to be observed on the first day of the week. Acts 20:7 records, "And upon the first day of the week when the disciples came together to break bread. . . ." When did the disciples come together to break bread? There is neither command, example, nor necessary inference for observing the Lord's supper any other day. If so, where is the passage? When there is no command, example, or necessary inference, there is no authority for such practice. To observe the Lord's supper any day other than the first day of the week is to show disrespect for the silence of the Scriptures and to tamper with the Word of God, which we are strictly forbidden to do (1 Cor. 4:6; 2 John 9; Rev. 22:18-19).

III. Had the Word of the Lord just said, "the disciples came together to break bread," then we would be at liberty to observe the Lord's supper any day. But, the Bible doesn't say that! The Bible rather says, "upon

24

the first day of the week." That is when, and only when, we are authorized to observe it.

FOR CLASS DISCUSSION:
1. Why do you think there are those who would want to observe the Lord's supper on a day other than the first day of the week?
2. Can you think of other days God has been specific about? Do you think the Lord's people could observe these days just any time they wanted?
3. What is the significance of the first day of the week?

ERROR: **Tithing Is the Scriptural Method of Gathering Money**

ANSWER:
I.   Tithing was an Old Testament command for the children of Israel (Lev. 27:30-34).
II.   For tithing to be binding today, the Old Testament would have to be binding. The Old Testament has been done away (Eph. 2:15; Col. 2:14; Heb. 8:7-13).
III.   If you're going to go back to the Old Testament and keep the tithing command, you are a "debtor to do the whole law" (Gal. 5:4). Offered your animal sacrifices? Been to Jerusalem to worship?
IV.   Since we live under "the law of Christ" (Gal. 6:2), we must look to New Testament teaching to learn the scriptural method of gathering money. The New Testament method just calls for Christians, upon the first day of the week, to "lay by him in store" (1 Cor. 16:1-2) and "Every man according as he purposeth in his heart, so let him give. . . ." (2 Cor. 9:7).

FOR CLASS DISCUSSION:
1. How will you reap if you sow sparingly (2 Cor. 9:6)?
2. Make a list of biblical examples of bountiful givers.
3. What may money given to the Lord scripturally be used for?

ERROR: **Infants Are Subjects of Bible Baptism**

ANSWER:
I.   Bible baptism is "for the remission of sins" (Acts 2:38). An infant does not need to be baptized for he has no sins (Ezek. 18:20; Mark 10:14-15; Col. 3:25).
II. Infants are not fit subjects of Bible baptism as they do not meet the requirements of Bible baptism. Baptism requires teaching (Matt. 28:19; John 6:44-45), hearing (Acts 2:37), faith (Mark 16:16; Acts 8:36-37), repentance (Luke 13:3; Acts 2:38), and a confession of one's faith in Christ (Acts 8:37; Rom. 10:9-10). A little baby cannot meet these requirements.
III. I read in the Bible where "both men and women" were baptized (Acts 8:12), but where do you ever read of infants being baptized?

FOR CLASS DISCUSSION:
1. How would you answer one who argues that the "household baptisms" support infant baptism?
2. Any idea how infant baptism got started in the first place?
3. When the New Testament talks about "sprinkling," what is under consideration (Heb. 11:28; 12:24; 1 Pet. 1:2)?

ERROR: **The Bible Is Not the Word of God**

ANSWER:
I.   The Bible claims to be of God. Paul affirmed, "All scripture is given by inspiration of God, and is profitable for doctrine, for reproof, for correction, for instruction in righteousness: That the man of God may be perfect, throughly furnished unto all good works" (2 Tim. 3:16-17). "Inspiration of God" means the Bible is God-breathed. The Bible is so verbally inspired that a writer made an argument on one letter of a word (1 Cor. 2:12-13; Gal. 3:16). Paul commended the Thessalonians for receiving the word "not as the word of men, but as it is in truth, the word of God" (1 Thess. 2:13). Peter penned, "For the prophecy came not in old time by the will of man: but holy men of God spake as they were moved by the Holy Ghost" (2 Pet. 1:21).
II. This claim is proven by: (1) **Its unity.** The Bible was written by about forty writers over a period of some 1600 years. They lived in different times and places, spoke different languages, and wrote on a variety of

subjects. Yet, their writings contain one harmonious message, without a single contradiction, discrepancy, or error. (2) **Its fulfilled prophecies.** The prophets of the Old Testament all looked into the centuries beyond and spoke with explicit detail of things to come with nothing in the present upon which to base their statements. Yet, when we read the New Testament, we can't help but be impressed with the fact that every one of their darts of prophecy is in the bull's eye! Consider, for example, Isaiah's prophecy concerning the establishment of the Lord's church in Isaiah 2 and its exact fulfillment in Acts 2. 3) **Its scientific foreknowledge.** The Bible is not a science book, but everything it says touching the field of science is scientifically accurate. Genesis 1:1-2 contains the five facts of science in scientific order. The Bible speaks of the rotundity of the earth (Is. 40:22), the rotation of the earth (Job 38:13-14), ocean boundary (Job 38:8, 11), aviation (Is. 60:8), and many other such facts. These facts were not discovered until centuries after the Bible was written. The only way these men could have written such is that God was guiding the pen of inspiration!

III. Since the Bible is the Word of God, we need to read, believe, and obey it! One of these days, we will be judged by it (John 12:48; Rom. 2:16).

FOR CLASS DISCUSSION:
1. How does 1 Corinthians 2:12-13 show God did not just put the thoughts in the minds of the writers and allow them to express those thoughts in their own words?
2. Discuss some other evidences that show the Bible is God's Word.
3. There are many alleged contradictions of the Bible. Find one and be prepared to explain that it is not a contradiction.

ERROR: **We Are Saved by Grace Alone**

ANSWER:
I. The Bible does teach we are saved by the grace of God (Eph. 2:8; Tit. 2:11), but where is the passage that teaches we are saved by grace alone?
II. This religious error makes salvation one-sided. If we are saved by grace alone, then God has done everything and man has no role to play in being saved. The Scriptures teach there are two sides to salva-

27

tion: God's and man's. Ephesians 2:8 says, "For by grace are ye saved through faith. ..." *Grace* is God's side. *Faith* is man's part. If man has nothing to do in being saved, why were those on Pentecost told, "Repent, and be baptized ... for the remission of sins," when they asked, "Men and brethren, what shall we do?" (Acts 2:37-38). Why was the jailor told, "Believe on the Lord Jesus Christ," when he asked, "What must I do to be saved?" (Acts 16:30-31).

III. Grace is just one of the many things by which we are saved. We are saved by faith (John 8:24), baptism (1 Pet. 3:21), the gospel (1 Cor. 15:1-2), preaching (1 Cor. 1:21), and so on. If all these save, then we are not saved by grace alone.

FOR CLASS DISCUSSION:
1. Show from Titus 2:11 that, if salvation is by grace alone, none will be lost.
2. The Bible teaches we are saved like Noah (1 Pet. 3:20-21). Was Noah saved by grace alone? What things were involved in the saving of Noah?
3. If we are saved by grace alone, then how could we fall from grace? How does Galatians 5:4 refute this false teaching?

ERROR: Jesus Was Just a Man

ANSWER:
I.   The Bible refers to Jesus as both the "Son of man" (Matt. 16:13) and the "Son of God" (Mark 1:1). He was both human and divine, while on earth.
II. Jesus claimed to be divine (John 9:33-37). Don't you think Jesus knew who He was?
III. Many acknowledged the deity of Jesus (Matt. 14:33; 16:16; Mark 3:11; 15:39; John 1:34, 49; 11:27; Acts 8:37; 9:20).

FOR CLASS DISCUSSION:
1. Show from John 1:1-3, 14 that Jesus was God in the flesh.
2. The differences in Jesus and men show that Jesus was more than just a man. How was Jesus different from ordinary men?
3. What does Philippians 2:5-8 teach?

ERROR: God Speaks Today Apart from the Bible

ANSWER:
I. The phrase "God hath spoken" shows God has said all that He intends to say (Heb. 1:1-2).
II. Jesus promised the apostles they would be guided into all truth (John 16:13). If God is still revealing truth, the apostles were not guided into all truth as Christ promised.
III. Paul said that he declared all the counsel of God (Acts 20:27). How could Paul have made such a claim, if God's message to man was not complete?
IV. Timothy was taught, "All scripture is given by inspiration of God, and is profitable for doctrine, for reproof, for correction, for instruction in righteousness: That the man of God may be perfect, throughly furnished unto all good works" (2 Tim. 3:16-17). The American Standard Version says, "that the man of God may be complete, furnished completely unto every good work." The fact that man may be complete shows the Word of God is complete. The Bible is all we need.
V. If God is still giving revelation, then Peter was mistaken when he said that God "hath given unto us all things that pertain unto life and godliness" (2 Pet. 1:3).
VI. The faith, which is the gospel (Col. 1:23), "was once delivered unto the saints" (Jude 3). That is, once for all time. Once a thing has been delivered, it does not need to be redelivered.

FOR CLASS DISCUSSION:
1. If God speaks to you in a special way apart from the Bible, but not me, that would make Him partial. How does Acts 10:34 answer this?
2. How may the warnings against adding to the Word of God be used in answering this error (1 Cor. 4:6; Gal. 1:8-9; 2 John 9; Rev. 22:18-19)?
3. It's not a matter of how God has spoken in time past. The question is, "How does God speak today?" Study Hebrews 1:1-4 and be prepared to discuss in class.

ERROR: Man Comes Back in Another Form After Death

ANSWER:
I.   Where in the Bible did the Lord ever say anything about reincarnation? Can you show an example in the Bible where anyone came back in another form after he died?
II. Upon his son's death, David said, "I shall go to him, but he shall not return to me" (2 Sam. 12:23). Once you're dead, there's no coming back (Job 7:9).
III. The Hebrew writer penned, "And as it is appointed unto men once to die, but after this the judgment" (Heb. 9:27). Man only dies once. If there is but one physical death, then there must be but one physical life. If not, why not?
IV. When a man dies, this is the end of his earthly existence. Solomon revealed concerning the dead, "neither have they any more a portion for ever in any thing that is done under the sun" (Eccl. 9:6).

FOR CLASS DISCUSSION:
1. Define reincarnation.
2. What are some consequences of this kind of thinking?
3. What does the Bible have to say about what happens after death?

ERROR: We Can't Understand the Bible

ANSWER:
I.   When Old Testament people read the law of God, they understood it. For example, "So they read in the book in the law of God distinctly, and gave the sense, and caused them to understand the reading" (Neh. 8:8).
II. Timothy was said to have "from a child known the holy scriptures which are able to make thee wise unto salvation" (2 Tim. 3:15). If Timothy could know the Scriptures from a child, then surely we can come to know and understand them as well.
III. Paul said we may understand the Bible. Ephesians 3:4 records, "Whereby, when ye read, ye may understand my knowledge in the mystery of Christ." It may be that we don't understand the Bible because we haven't read it enough.
IV. God expects us to understand His will. "Wherefore be ye not unwise, but understanding what the will of the Lord is" (Eph. 5:17).

V. Do you think God would give us a book containing His will for us, command us to read and understand it, and then make it too difficult to understand?

FOR CLASS DISCUSSION:
1. Sometimes we may not have the proper understanding of the Bible, because we haven't learned how to study it. What are some basic rules of Bible study?
2. How often should one read and study the Bible, and how do you think this would affect one's understanding?
3. Why do you think some would want folks to believe they can't understand the Bible?

ERROR: Man Does Not Have an Immortal Soul

ANSWER:
I.   This religious error stems from a misunderstanding of the word "soul." Sometimes "soul" refers to the entire individual as "eight souls were saved by water" (1 Pet. 3:20). The word "soul" is also used in reference to the part of man that is immortal. A good example is when Peter said, "Seeing ye have purified your souls in obeying the truth..." (1 Pet. 1:22). What does a person purify when he obeys the truth? Certainly not the physical body. Peter declared, "not the putting away of the filth of the flesh" (1 Pet. 3:21). The words "soul" and "spirit" are sometimes used interchangeably in the Bible (Acts 2:27-31; Luke 23:46).
II. The Bible teaches that man is composed of body and spirit. "For ye are bought with a price: therefore glorify God in your body, and in your spirit, which are God's" (1 Cor. 6:20). "And fear not them which kill the body, but are not able to kill the soul: but rather fear him which is able to destroy both soul and body in hell" (Matt. 10:28).
III. The soul can depart the body. The death of Rachel shows her soul left her when she died. "And it came to pass, as her soul was in departing, (for she died)..." (Gen. 35:18). The soul of a widow's son came back into his body. "...and the soul of the child came into him again, and he revived" (1 Kings 17:22). James shows us this great truth when he said, "For as the body without the spirit is dead, so faith without works is dead also" (James 2:26). Physical death occurs when the spirit departs the body. Only the body dies. The spirit lives on as it goes back "unto God who gave it" (Eccl. 12:7).

31

IV. We are two men. In 2 Corinthians 4:16-18, Paul compares the outward man with the inward man. The outward man is the physical body. The inward man is the spirit. Notice some differences in these two men:

Outward Man	Inward Man
Perishing	Renewed
Visible	Invisible
Temporal	Eternal

FOR CLASS DISCUSSION:
1. How does the story of Luke 16:19-31 answer this religious error?
2. Suppose one brought in passages like Ecclesiastes 3:19-20 and 9:5, how would you handle this?
3. If man does not have an immortal soul, then when he dies he is dead all over. Be prepared to show from Matthew 22:32 that this is not the case.

ERROR: **God Chose Certain Ones to Be Lost or Saved, Without Involving Their Choice in the Matter**

ANSWER:
I.   If this be true, then God is partial. If I can prove God is not partial, then I have proved this doctrine to be false. Proof abounds of the impartiality of God (Acts 10:34-35; Rom. 2:11; Eph. 6:9; Col. 3:25; 1 Pet. 1:17).
II. God did not choose the individual to be saved, but He rather chose the place where men are saved. God chose us in Christ (Eph. 1:3-6), and salvation is in Christ (2 Tim. 2:10). Those in Christ are predestined to be saved. Those outside of Christ are predestined to be lost. Whether I get into Christ or not, by being baptized (Gal. 3:27), is entirely up to me.
III. All are invited to come unto the Lord (Matt. 11:28; Rev. 22:17). Why are all invited, if all cannot come? Many fail to accept the invitation, but that's not God's fault.
IV. If certain ones will be lost or saved and they have no choice in the matter, then Jesus died for a select few. To the contrary, the Bible teaches Jesus died "for every man" (Heb. 2:9). John said, "And he is the propitiation for our sins: and not for ours only, but also for the sins of the whole world" (1 John 2:2).

32

V. Folks will be lost, not because God chose them to be lost, but because they chose not to obey God (2 Thess. 1:8).

FOR CLASS DISCUSSION:
1. Does the Bible teach predestination? If so, where and in what way does it teach it?
2. Find some examples in the Bible which show that man is a creature possessing the power to choose.
3. Have you ever met one who was predestined to be lost? You would think that as many as are going to be lost (Matt. 7:13-14, 21-23), you would eventually run into a person God chose to be lost, wouldn't you?

ERROR: **The Holy Spirit Operates Directly on Man, Apart from the Bible**

ANSWER:
I. If the Holy Spirit operates directly on man today, apart from the Word of God, then the Bible would not be all-sufficient. The Bible is all we need (2 Tim. 3:16-17).
II. Every influence the Holy Spirit is said to have upon man, the Word of God is said to accomplish the same thing. This shows that the Word is the medium through which the Holy Spirit operates upon man today. Note some examples: Spiritual begetting (James 1:18; 1 Cor. 4:15), spiritual birth (1 Pet. 1:23), quickening of the heart (Col. 2:12-13; Ps. 119:50), cleansing of the soul (John 15:2; Eph. 5:26), purification of the soul (1 Pet. 1:22), saving of the soul (James 1:21-22), justification process (Rom. 2:13), means of guidance (Ps. 73:24; 119:1-5), growth of the child of God (1 Pet. 2:2), bringing forth of fruit (Gal. 5:22-25; Col. 1:5-6), source of spiritual strength (Acts 20:32), comforting of the bereaved (1 Thess. 4:18), and the work of sanctification (John 17:17; Eph. 5:26). **Now this question:** If the Holy Spirit operates directly upon man, apart from the Word of God, just what does He do that is not affirmed of the Word?

FOR CLASS DISCUSSION:
1. Show from Ephesians 6:17 and Acts 2:37 that the Holy Spirit influences man today through the medium of the Word of God.

2. When we point out that the Holy Spirit works through the Word, some want to bring up Romans 8:16. What is this passage teaching?
3. The Holy Spirit dwells in the child of God (1 Tim. 1:14). Show from Ephesians 5:18 and Colossians 3:16, parallel passages, that the Spirit of God dwells representatively through the Word of God and not personally, apart from the Bible.

ERROR: God Is Still Working Miracles Today

ANSWER:
I.   This belief comes from a misuse of the word "miracle." These are not miracles: Any unusual happening, things which are coincidental, something unexplainable, or the providence of God. Calling a thing a miracle makes it a miracle, no more than calling a dog a hog makes it a pig! A miracle is a demonstration of supernatural intervention either directly upon an object or person, or through some person or agent, in which no natural force is responsible for the effect produced.
II. Miracles have served their purpose and are no longer needed. Miracles, in the New Testament, confirmed the certainty of the truth taught by the one performing them. The miracles of Jesus established the truthfulness of His claim to be the Son of God (Matt. 11:2-5). There is no need for folks today to see a miracle to believe that Jesus is the Son of God. We have all the evidence needed in the recorded testimony of competent witnesses (John 20:30-31). The miracles of the apostles confirmed the truthfulness of the Word preached (Mark 16:14-20; Heb. 2:3-4). Since the Word of God has already been confirmed, there is no need for miracles today to confirm it. The miracles of those endowed with spiritual gifts confirmed the Word as it was revealed through prophets to edify the church in the absence of complete revelation (1 Cor. 14:12). Now that the faith has been "once delivered to the saints" (Jude 3), there is no need for the working of miracles. **Now this question:** If God is still working miracles, as He did in Bible days, what is the purpose of these miracles?
III. Miraculous activity has failed, ceased, and vanished away (1 Cor. 13:8-12).
IV. The absence of miracles proves God is no longer working miracles. Have you ever seen a rod turned into a serpent, water turned into wine, or the dead raised?
V.   If you believe to possess miraculous ability as our Lord and His apos-

tles, we would be glad to let you prove this claim by bringing a dead one back to life. Would you like to go to the cemetery? As brother Foy E. Wallace, Jr. once said, "As goes the proposition, so must be the demonstration!"

FOR CLASS DISCUSSION:
1. God began things with a miracle and they continue through law. Can you think of some examples?
2. Contrast the miracles of the Bible with the so-called miracles of to-day.
3. Study the miraculous raising of dead Lazarus in Luke 11 and learn the effect it produced.

ERROR: Just as Long as You're a Good Person, Nothing Else Matters

ANSWER:
I. Being a good person is important (Tit. 2:12), but you will not get to heaven on good behavior alone.
II. Many good people will be lost (Matt. 7:21-23).
III. Cornelius was a good man. He is described as, "A devout man, and one that feared God with all his house, which gave much alms to the people, and prayed to God alway" (Acts 10:2). Yet, he was not saved for he had to hear words whereby he could be saved (Acts 11:14). It takes more than goodness alone to save a person!
IV. We must obey Christ to be saved for He is "the author of eternal salvation unto all them that obey him" (Heb. 5:9). An individual may be a good person, but when it comes to obedience be weighed in the balances and found wanting.

FOR CLASS DISCUSSION:
1. Many of the conversions in the book of Acts involved people who were religious. Provide some examples.
2. Since "faith cometh by hearing, and hearing by the word of God" (Rom. 10:17), if Cornelius was saved by morality alone, then what would he have been saved without (Acts 11:14)?
3. If just being a good person is not enough, then what must a person do to be saved?

ERROR: Calling the Preacher Pastor, Reverend, Bishop, Father, Etc.

ANSWER:

I.   The terms "bishop" and "pastor" refer to elders in the church, not preachers. Paul told the Ephesian elders, "Take heed therefore unto yourselves, and to all the flock, over the which the Holy Ghost hath made you overseers (bishops), to feed (pastor) the church of God, which he hath purchased with his own blood" (Acts 20:17, 28).

II. "Reverend" is found only one time in the Bible. The word is used in reference to God and not a preacher. It is said of God, "holy and reverend is his name" (Ps. 111:9).

III. The Lord said, "But be not ye called Rabbi: for one is your Master, even Christ; and all ye are brethren. And call no man your father upon the earth: for one is your Father, which is in heaven. Neither be ye called masters: for one is your Master, even Christ" (Matt. 23:8-11). There is no clergy-laity distinction in the Bible.

IV. Job declared, "Let me not, I pray you, accept any man's person, neither let me give flattering titles unto man. For I know not to give flattering titles; in so doing my maker would soon take me away" (Job 32:21-22).

FOR CLASS DISCUSSION:

1.   Religious titles are designed to elevate a man. What did Paul have to say about this in 1 Corinthians 4:6?

2.   What are the scriptural designations of preachers?

3.   Could these scriptural designations be used unscripturally? If so, how?

ERROR: Sabbath Keeping Is Still Binding Today

ANSWER:

I.   Sabbath keeping belonged to the Jewish dispensation (Exod. 20:8). For the Sabbath to be binding today, the Old Testament would have to be binding. The law of Moses, which included the Sabbath command, has been done away (Col. 2:14-17).

II. The Sabbath command was given to fleshly Israel (Exod. 20:1-2; 31:12-13, 16-17; Deut. 4:8; 5:1-3, 6, 15). If you keep the Sabbath day, were you among those brought out of Egypt?

III. If the Sabbath day is still binding, then in order to keep the Sabbath properly, you would have to do no servile work (Exod. 35:1-3; Num. 15:32-36), offer a burnt offering (Num. 28:9-10), kindle no fire (Exod. 35:3), and not go out of your place (Exod. 16:29). Do you do this?
IV. Keeping the Sabbath day makes one a "debtor to do the whole law" (Gal. 5:3). If you keep the Sabbath, do you burn incense, offer animal sacrifices, and go to Jerusalem to worship three times in the year?
V. We live under "the law of Christ" (Gal. 6:2) and are bound to keep the "first day of the week" (Acts 20:7; 1 Cor. 16:1-2). In the New Testament, there is no command to keep the Sabbath day and no penalty for not keeping it.

FOR CLASS DISCUSSION:
1. Why did God command Israel to keep the Sabbath day (Deut. 5:15)?
2. Why did Israel keep the Sabbath before the law was given (Exod. 16)?
3. Is Sunday the Christian Sabbath?

ERROR: Observing Special Religious Holidays

ANSWER:
I. The Lord said to, "observe all things whatsoever I have commanded you" (Matt. 28:20). Where is the Scripture that commands the religious observance of special holidays?
II. The church worships as Christ directs (Col. 1:18; Matt. 15:9). The worship consists of breaking of bread and giving on each first day of the week, accompanied by teaching, praying, and singing (Acts 2:42; Eph. 5:19). Every Sunday is alike in this regard. In observing special religious holidays, such as Christmas and Easter, about all churches include as acts of worship activities not even mentioned in the Bible.
III. Paul said, "Ye observe days, and months, and times, and years. I am afraid of you, lest I have bestowed upon you labour in vain" (Gal. 4:10-11).

FOR CLASS DISCUSSION:
1. Discuss some of the holidays observed in the religious world today and their various activities.
2. How should the non-religious observance of Christmas, Easter, and the like as national holidays be treated?

3. Did the Lord's people in the New Testament ever have trouble over the observance of days, and if so what kind of trouble did they have?

ERROR: **The Second Coming of Christ, Including the Establishment of the Eternal Kingdom, the Day of Judgment, the End of the World, and the Resurrection of the Dead All Occurred in A.D. 70.**

ANSWER:

I. Christ has not yet come. John recorded, "Behold, he cometh with clouds; and every eye shall see him" (Rev. 1:7). Have you ever seen the Lord? If Christ has already come, there would be no reason for observing the Lord's supper. Its purpose is to "shew the Lord's death till he come" (1 Cor. 11:26). Do you observe the Lord's supper? If Christ came in A.D. 70, then every person has been eternally rewarded. "For the Son of man shall come in the glory of his Father with his angels; and then he shall reward every man according to his works" (Matt. 16:27). Did you get your reward?

II. The kingdom was in existence before A.D. 70. The saints at Colosse were said to be in the kingdom (Col. 1:13). Paul's letter to the Colossians was written about ten years before A.D. 70! Daniel's prophecy of the establishment of the kingdom (Dan. 2:44; 7:13-14) was fulfilled in Acts 2, when "the Lord added to the church daily such as should be saved" (Acts 2:47). This occurred about forty years before A.D. 70!

III. The judgment, the end of the world, and the resurrection of the dead will all take place at the last day. Martha said concerning Lazarus, "I know that he shall rise again in the resurrection at the last day" (John 11:24). If the resurrection occurred in A.D. 70, then that would have been the last day, but there have been over 704,000 days since. When the resurrection comes, "all that are in the graves shall hear his voice, and shall come forth..." (John 5:28-29). Every time a body is exhumed from mother earth it is added proof that the dead are still in the graves! When the end comes, the world will be burned up (2 Pet. 3:10-11). To understand that the world did not end in A.D. 70, one has but to look around and see that the world still turns. The judgment is yet future. Jesus said, "He that rejecteth me, and receiveth not my words, hath one that judgeth him: the word that I have spoken, the same shall judge him in the last day" (John 12:48). The fact that days still come and go shows the judgment has not taken place yet and we still need to ready ourselves for it.

FOR CLASS DISCUSSION:
1. Make a study of some things the Bible teaches concerning the Lord's second coming.
2. What do the Scriptures have to say about the judgment?
3. What will take place when the end comes?

ERROR: **The Doctrine of Transubstantiation (The Bread and Fruit of the Vine in the Lord's Supper Become the Literal Body and Blood of Jesus)**

ANSWER:
I. This religious error comes from a literal interpretation of Matthew 26:26, 28. Jesus said of the bread, "This is my body" and of the cup, "This is my blood." These statements must be interpreted figuratively as Jesus was actually present in flesh and blood when He said these things. Jesus also said He was "bread" (John 6:48), "light" (John 8:12), a "door" (John 10:7), a "vine" (John 15:1), and many other things that must be taken figuratively. To understand these statements literally is but to misunderstand them!
II. A misuse of John 6:53-58 has caused some to believe the transubstantiation doctrine. John 6 has no reference whatsoever to the Lord's supper. To use it in connection with the Lord's supper is to misuse it! If eating His flesh means taking the Lord's supper, then everyone who eats of the bread receives eternal life (John 6:51). The words of Christ are under consideration as the Lord said, "It is the spirit that quickeneth; the flesh profiteth nothing: the words that I speak unto you, they are spirit, and they are life" (John 6:63).
III. The cup of blessing represents the blood of Christ and the bread represents the body of Christ (1 Cor. 10:16). No matter what any man says or does, the bread and fruit of the vine do not become the literal body and blood of Jesus.

FOR CLASS DISCUSSION:
1. Make a list of Scripture references where one can read about the Lord's supper.
2. Discuss what it means to discern the Lord's body from 1 Corinthians 11:29.

39

3. Show that the observance of the Lord's supper is both a collective and personal affair.

ERROR: **Continual Cleansing**

ANSWER:
I. If a Christian's sins are continually cleansed by the blood of Christ, without any conditions on his part, why then was Simon told to "repent" and "pray" for forgiveness in Acts 8:22?
II. If the doctrine of continual cleansing be so, why was the church at Corinth admonished to "put away" the brother that had his father's wife (1 Cor. 5:1-13)? Wouldn't the blood of Christ have taken care of that?
III. Why withdraw from the disorderly (2 Thess. 3:6), if they are continually cleansed by the blood of Christ without any actions on their part? There would be no need for church discipline, if this teaching be true.
IV. If this be so, then we could live any way we want to, without regard for the will of the Lord, and go to heaven when we die. In light of Titus 2:12, who can believe this?
V. The Bible teaches that the cleansing of a Christian's sins is conditional. John wrote, "But if we walk in the light, as he is in the light, we have fellowship one with another, and the blood of Jesus Christ his Son cleanseth us from all sin" (1 John 1:7). When are our sins cleansed? Verse 9 answers, "If we confess our sins, he is faithful and just to forgive us our sins, and to cleanse us from all unrighteousness." Our sins are cleansed when we confess our sins. Suppose a Christian doesn't confess his sins? No confessing, no cleansing. It's just that simple.

FOR CLASS DISCUSSION:
1. What is God's law of pardon for the alien sinner?
2. How does a child of God go about having his sins removed?
3. If this be true, looks like once you're saved, you're always saved. Show that the Bible doesn't teach this principle.

40

ERROR: Romans 14 Includes Moral and Doctrinal Differences

ANSWER:

I.   One of the basic rules of Bible study is that the Bible must harmonize. Whatever Romans 14 says must be consistent with everything else the Bible says about fellowship. To make Romans 14 teach something contradictory to other plain passages of Scripture on the subject of fellowship is to make it teach something it does not teach!

II. The Bible teaches two different concepts concerning fellowship. (1) When a thing is a matter of sin, we are to "put away" that person (1 Cor. 5:13), or if a thing be a matter of false doctrine, John said, "receive him not" (2 John 9-11). In matters of sin or false doctrine, we can not have fellowship. (2) Where disagreements occur, but no sin or false teaching is involved, we are to "receive" one another (Rom. 14:1-15:7; 1 Cor. 10:19-33). We must not divide over personal scruples, authorized liberties, or matters of judgment; we are to have fellowship.

III. Romans 14 cannot include sinful or doctrinal matters, for the things under discussion in this chapter are things where we may differ and still receive our brother, "for God hath received him" (Rom. 14:3). The things under discussion in Romans 14 concern things that are clean, "nothing unclean of itself" (Rom. 14:14), and things that are pure, "All things indeed are pure" (Rom. 14:20). This means we must discern between things that are clean and unclean, pure and impure, right and wrong, lawful and sinful. If a thing is clean, pure, right, lawful, apply Romans 14. If it is unclean, impure, wrong, unlawful, then apply 2 John 9-11.

FOR CLASS DISCUSSION:

1. What instructions are given to the strong in Romans 14? What instructions are given to the weak?
2. Who is the strong? Who is the weak?
3. Show that matters of sin or false doctrine do not fit the teachings of Romans 14.

ERROR: Men Today Receive Holy Spirit Baptism

ANSWER:

I.   The baptism of the Holy Spirit was administered by Christ (Matt. 3:11). This passage shows who would administer it, not who would receive it. If men today receive Holy Spirit baptism, it would have to be administered directly by the Lord and not man.

II. Holy Spirit baptism was a promise, not a command (John 14:16). You will not find an example anywhere in the Bible where God ever commanded anyone to be baptized with the Holy Spirit. If so, where is the Scripture?

III. Those who believe this fail to realize to whom the baptism of the Holy Spirit was promised. It was promised to the apostles, not all men in general (Luke 24:49; John 14:16; Acts 1:2-8). The purpose was to guide them into all truth (John 14:26; 16:13).

IV. The promise of Holy Spirit baptism was received by the apostles on Pentecost (Acts 1:26-2:4). Only the apostles received the baptism of the Holy Spirit on Pentecost.

V.   The baptism of the Holy Spirit was received by the Gentiles, in a special instance, as recorded in Acts 10-11. The purpose of Holy Spirit baptism upon the Gentiles was for the benefit of the Jews to convince them, "Then hath God also to the Gentiles granted repentance unto life" (Acts 11:18). Men today do not receive Holy Spirit baptism for they were not promised it, and if they did, what purpose would it serve?

VI. At the time Paul wrote the Ephesians, he said there is "one baptism" (Eph. 4:5). If you have both water baptism and Holy Spirit baptism as being valid today, then you have one baptism too many.

FOR CLASS DISCUSSION:

1.   What did the baptism of the Holy Spirit enable the apostles to do?
2.   Show from Acts 10-11 that the baptism of the Holy Spirit had nothing to do with saving Cornelius.
3.   What does the Bible teach about the one baptism of Ephesians 4:5?

ERROR: Institutionalism

ANSWER:

I.   An institution is a corporate body, an established society or corporation. There are two types of institutions: Human and divine. "Institutionalism" is a term used in reference to the support of human institutions, such as orphan's homes in the work of benevolence, colleges in the work of edification, and missionary societies in the work of evangelism, from the church treasury.

II. Where in the Bible did one church ever send money to a human institution or another church somewhere in doing the work of gospel preaching? I read where the church sent funds directly to the preacher as Paul said, "No church communicated with me as concerning giving and receiving, but ye only. For even in Thessalonica ye sent once and again unto my necessity" (Phil. 4:15-16). There was no human missionary society or sponsoring church arrangement that stood between the church at Philippi and the apostle Paul.

III. In the matter of benevolence, it is not a matter of how the work is to be done (the place, the provisions, and the personnel), but who is charged with the responsibility of doing the work. In the New Testament, the local church took care of its own needy (Acts 2, 4, 6). When a church had a need greater than its ability to relieve, churches in other places, that had the ability to help in that need, sent to the elders of the congregation in need (Acts 11:27-30). Where did the Lord's people ever turn over this work to another institution of some kind to decide the place, provisions, and personnel, and contribute money from its treasury to support that institution?

IV. Where is Bible authority for elders overseeing any work other than that which is among them (Acts 20:28; 1 Pet. 5:1-2)?

V. Ephesians 4:7-8, 11-16 shows the all-sufficient design of the Lord's church. Whatever the Lord wants us to do collectively, He has provided all the information and organization necessary to do it. Institutionalism denies the all-sufficiency of the church. If God gave the church work to do, don't you think that, since He is the designer of the church (Eph. 3:11), He would have given everything necessary for the church to do that work? To say another organization is needed is to say the church is not all-sufficient, and such is an insult to the wisdom of God.

VI. The Lord's church was so successful, without other agencies, in spreading the gospel, that, in a very short period of time, Paul could say, "the gospel, which ye have heard, and which was preached to every creature which is under heaven" (Col. 1:23).

FOR CLASS DISCUSSION:
1. Give, in a nutshell, the organization of the Lord's church.
2. What work has the Lord charged the church to do?
3. Can you name some human institutions and sponsoring church arrangements?

ERROR: **Women Preachers, Elders, Deacons, and the Like**

ANSWER:
I. Where is the Scripture that authorizes a woman to preach the gospel? Can you name a woman preacher of the New Testament? For a woman to preach is to violate the teaching of Paul in 1 Timothy 2:11-14.
II. A woman cannot scripturally serve as an elder for she is not qualified. The qualifications, according to 1 Timothy 3:1-7, state: "If a man desire the office of a bishop, he desireth a good work." This "man" qualification eliminates the woman.
III. A woman cannot scripturally serve the church as a deacon for she cannot meet the qualifications given in 1 Timothy 3:8-13. Do you know any women who are "the husbands of one wife" (1 Tim. 3:12)? The woman can be a deacon no more than she can be a husband!
IV. The woman is out of her God-assigned place anytime she usurps "authority over the man" (1 Tim. 2:12).

FOR CLASS DISCUSSION:
1. What is the place of women?
2. According to 1 Timothy 2:13-14, why did God assign the woman this place?
3. Make a list of things women can do to promote the cause of Christ.

ERROR: **Evolution**

ANSWER:
I. Evolution theorizes that all things began in a single non-sex cell and that all phases, forms, and grades of life that now exist evolved and developed from a single cell. Evolutionists claim the original cell was a non-sex cell and upon millions of years it accidentally divided itself and became a dual cell, male and female.
II. If this be true, then where did that "single non-sex cell" come from? What produced it? How did it come into existence?

44

III. To say man evolved from a lower order of life through millions upon millions or even billions of years is to leave out the existence of his soul. If man developed from a lower animal, when did the soul enter into him? It couldn't have been there in his original state of development or his evolvement from a lower order of animals.
IV. The Bible reveals the origin of man. Man is the result of direct creation. God created man male and female (Gen. 1-2; Matt. 19:4). There's just no way you can believe the Bible and hold to the theory of evolution!
V. Evolution is at variance with the Bible from stem to stern! Evolution denies that life was created (Gen. 1). Evolution denies that God created man male and female (Gen. 1:26-27). Evolution denies that man is the unique creation of God, distinct from the animals (Gen. 1:26-27; Ps. 8:3-6). Evolution denies the fixity of the kinds in Genesis 1. Evolution overlooks the difference between human and animal blood (Acts 17:26). Evolution has water animals before land plants and reptiles before birds. Read Genesis 1 to see the proper order of these.

FOR CLASS DISCUSSION:
1. Be prepared to show how the Bible teaches things began.
2. Show from Genesis 1-3 that when man was created, God made him an intelligent being.
3. Can you think of other ways of answering this religious error?

ERROR: **Tongue Speaking Is Possible Today**

ANSWER:
I. Bible tongue speaking was the supernatural ability to speak a language which you did not know and had never studied (Acts 2:1-11). The only way men today speak a language is if they are taught or study and learn that language.
II. No man today has the ability to speak in tongues as was done in New Testament days, for the means of receiving this supernatural ability has been cut off. Bible tongue speaking was associated with the baptism of the Holy Spirit (Acts 2:1-4; 10:44-46). Since men today do not receive the baptism of the Holy Spirit, as it was only promised to the apostles (John 14:16-17; 16:13; Acts 1:4-8), tongue speaking is not possible today. Bible tongue speaking was one of the nine spiritual gifts of 1 Corinthians 12:8-10. These supernatural gifts could only be bestowed through "laying on of the apostles' hands" (Acts 8:14-18;

19:6). Since there are no living apostles today to impart these spiritual gifts, for no one meets the qualifications (Acts 1:21-22), tongue speaking is not possible today.

III. The so-called "tongue speaking" being done today bears no resemblance whatsoever to Bible tongue speaking. Bible tongue speaking was designed to be understood. Please read 1 Corinthians 14, noting the emphasis placed upon understanding. Tongue speaking today is a bunch of gibber jabber that is anything but understandable! Bible tongue speaking was also orderly. Read 1 Corinthians 14:27, 33, and 40 to observe this orderly rule. Tongue speaking today is about as orderly as Metro Manila traffic!

IV. No matter the claim, no man alive today has the ability to speak in tongues as was done in the Bible.

FOR CLASS DISCUSSION:
1. Show from Acts 2:6-8 that tongues were languages.
2. How does 1 Corinthians 13:8 answer this religious error?
3. When did this supernatural ability cease?

ERROR: The Rapture

ANSWER:
I. The rapture theory is a period of time before a great period of trouble comes, when the saints of God will be caught up from the earth to escape their earthly troubles. The rapture people also tell us that when this troubled time is over, the saints will come back to earth to reign with Christ a thousand years in an earthly kingdom.

II. A reason for this false theory being taught is due to a misunderstanding of 1 Thessalonians 4:13-17, 1 Corinthians 15:51-52, and Matthew 24.

III. Rapture theory people misunderstand the phrase, "And the dead in Christ shall rise first" in 1 Thessalonians 4:13-17. The question that needs to be asked is, "The dead shall rise first before whom?" Then, it becomes a simple matter of reading the context. The dead in Christ will rise first, before the living rise.

IV. Those believing the rapture theory will read the statement, "we shall all be changed, in a moment, in the twinkling of an eye" in 1 Corinthians 15:51-52 and think of it as the rapture. A reading of the chapter will show the subject is the resurrection, not the rapture!

46